SATAN
THE GREAT IDENTITY THIEF

By
GENE AUTRY RHODES

Copyright © 2015 by Gene Autry Rhodes

Satan The Great Identity Thief
by Gene Autry Rhodes

Printed in the United States of America

ISBN 9781498424059

All rights reserved solely by the author. The author guarantees all contents are original and do not infringe upon the legal rights of any other person or work. No part of this book may be reproduced in any form without the permission of the author. The views expressed in this book are not necessarily those of the publisher.

Unless otherwise indicated, Scripture quotations are taken from the King James Version (KJV) – public domain: The Amplified Bible (AMP). Copyright © 1954, 1958, 1962, 1964, 1965, 1987 by The Lockman Foundation. Used by permission. All rights reserved.

www.xulonpress.com

DEDICATION

I dedicate this book to my loving supportive wife, Lady Elnora Heyward Rhodes. You believed in me and constantly encouraged me to finish this project. Your love brings out the best in me, and because of you, godly favor reigns in my life. Never allow Satan to steal your identity in Christ. To God be the glory! Amen.

Table of Contents

Acknowledgements ix
Introduction: Satan—The Great Identity Thief xi

Chapter 1:   Legal View 15
Chapter 2:   Sexual Mine Field 21
Chapter 3:   Drinking Your Identity Away 34
Chapter 4:   Suicide 39
Chapter 5:   Pride and Arrogance 45
Chapter 6:   Hypocrisy (Two Faces) 49
Chapter 7:   Domestic Violence (Love That Hurts) 54
Chapter 8:   Hamartiology 58
Chapter 9:   Demonology 61
Chapter 10: Christology 66
Chapter 11: Soteriology 75
Chapter 12: Eschatology 80
Chapter 13: Think—A Brain Snack 84

Bibliography of References 89
About The Author 91

Acknowledgements

First, I would like to thank my Heavenly Father for putting this gift within me, and now allowing it to be shared with the world.

Love and thanks to my pastors, Bishop James and Dr. Cynthia Bolden, of the Evangelistic Ministries Church, Jacksonville, Arkansas, for your support.

Definitely need to say thank you to my mom, (the late) Addie Rhodes, and my dad, Eugene Rhodes for encouraging us to surpass their achievements in life.

Thanks to my Spiritual Fathers in ministry, Rev. Lawrence Echols, Sr., of Blytheville, Arkansas, and Bishop Stanford L. Butts of Mitchellville, Maryland.

Thanks to Pastor Willie R. Hunt of Waldorf, Maryland for teaching me about 5:00 a.m. prayer, it still works.

A very special thank you to all who have sown seeds in my life. Know that from the depths of my heart you are appreciated and not forgotten. Thanks and God bless.

Introduction

Satan—The Great Identity Theft

Identity theft is one of the fastest growing crimes not only in the United States, but in the world. Its effects are of global proportion. Identity theft does not discriminate. It preys upon the weak as well as the strong, the poor as well as the rich. As a matter of fact, the identity thief is not concerned about your well-being, therefore he or she leaves a trail of emotional, physical, and financial chaos, never looking back to see the destruction he or she caused. They go about covertly acquiring your personal information and using it for medical services, credit accounts, or some other scheme they have in mind for financial gains. All of this activity is executed against your prior knowledge or authorization for use of your personal sensitive information, and you do not profit from any of it.

> *Identity theft is cruel, cold, vicious, and downright thoughtless.*

Identity theft is cruel, cold, vicious, and downright thoughtless.

It leaves one to ponder what type of person would do this to another human being. The actions of the identity thief are synonymous with the actions of Satan, who the word of God refers to as a thief who comes to steal, kill, and destroy (John 10:10).

Emotional, Physical, and Financial Distress

Although the human identity thief is not thinking he or she is actually hurting anyone, nothing can be further from the truth. When you steal from someone, it causes emotional, physical, and financial distress. Just because the thief does not sense nor realize the damage of his or her deeds does not mean that anything traumatic did not happen.

First of all, there is the **emotional distress** involved in having your personal space violated. A disgusted feeling of knowing someone entered your private sanctuary and has taken something of precious value from you that you strongly cherish. Now you must improve the security of your sanctuary to prevent or deter those who would try again.

Second point, there is **physical stress** on the body. I know because I have experienced the loss of sound sleep when my private sanctuary was violated. There are still times I think I hear things throughout the night making it impossible for me to rest. I awakened physically and mentally fatigued.

Then, there are thoughts of revenge that go round and round in your mind. These thoughts of wanting to physically lay hands on the one or ones responsible can cause both mental and physical stress. I had to learn to channel that anger for good and not bad although my flesh wanted to do bodily harm or seek some other form of revenge on the perpetrators.

Finally, the **financial distress** of losing items that are irreplaceable. These items hold great sentimental value to the owner, but are merely the means of making a quick buck to the thief. Consequently, the thief does not care about any of that, but is only concerned about the money those items can produce for them.

Steal, Kill, and Destroy

If a person will steal, the potential is there that they will also kill.

Not all thefts go according to the thief's original plans. Business or home owners return unexpectedly forcing the thief to improvise in order to escape. That escape route might mean going through the owner of the property, prompting the thief to make drastic decisions. Although the thief may have not intended for anyone to get injured, the property owner may not be willing to let the thief get out without

> *If a person will steal, the potential is there that they will also kill.*

a fight for those personal possessions. At this point theft may turn to murder.

Although identity theft is a growing crime in the natural, Satan has been using it much longer than we have noticed. Satan has tried to steal man's identity from the beginning of creation. Though his plan started strong, he has failed miserably. However, he is not willing to give up until his time is up so it is important for us to learn how Satan's tactics are used to try and achieve identity theft. We must always be watchful when dealing with Satan just as we must be with credit scores and other personal sensitive data. God's word tells us to be sober and vigilant because our enemy, Satan, goes about like a roaring lion looking for someone to devour (1 Peter 5:8).

⸎ Key Points to Remember

- ⸎ Identity theft is cruel, cold, vicious, and downright thoughtless.
- ⸎ If a person will steal, the potential is there that they will also kill.
- ⸎ God refers to Satan as a thief who comes to steal, kill, and destroy (John 10:10).
- ⸎ We must be sober and vigilant because our enemy, Satan, goes about like a roaring lion looking for someone to devour (1 Peter 5:8).

Chapter 1
Legal View

According to the Justice Department, identity theft is a crime. Identity theft and identity fraud are terms used to refer to all types of crime in which someone wrongfully obtains and uses another person's personal data in some way that involves fraud or deception for economic gain. Unlike your fingerprints which are unique to you and cannot be given to someone else for their use, your personal data, especially your Social Security Number, your bank account number, credit card number, telephone number, and other valuable identifying data can be used if they fall into the wrong hands.

> *The primary objective of the identity thief is to personally profit at your expense without a hint of remorse or regret for your loss.*

The primary objective of the identity thief is to personally profit at your expense without a hint of remorse or regret for your loss.

Unauthorized persons have taken funds out of bank or financial accounts, taken over identities, run up vast debts, and committed crimes while using the names of their victims. In many cases, a victim's losses may include not only out-of-pocket financial losses, but substantial additional financial costs associated with trying to restore their reputation in the community, and correcting erroneous misinformation for which the criminal is responsible.

The Federal Trade Commission (FTC) states that identity theft happens when someone steals your personal information and uses it without your permission, and can wreak what seems like insurmountable havoc on your life. The victims of identity theft can suffer adverse consequences if they are held accountable for the perpetrator's actions. Receiving phone calls and messages seeking payment for services they did not request or enjoy while their credit suffers from this wrongful malicious act can be quite stressful. The additional cost of legal fees increases the weight of the burden of restoring their good name.

The term identity theft was coined in 1964, but other terms like identity fraud or impersonation are also used to refer to this crime. Determining the link between data breaches and identity theft is very challenging, primarily because victims often do not know how their personal information was obtained.

Identity theft is often divided into five categories to help track information on the various ways identity theft is committed:

A. Criminal Identity Theft—posing as another person when apprehended for a crime.
B. Financial Identity Theft—using another's identity to obtain credit, goods, or services.
C. Identity Cloning—using another's information to assume his/her identity in daily life.
D. Medical Identity Theft—using another's identity to obtain medical care or drugs.
E. Child Identity Theft—using the child's Social Security Number for personal gain. Children Social Security Numbers are of high value to the identity thief because they do not have any information associated with them, thereby easily establishing lines of credit, obtaining driver licenses, or even buy a house using the child's identity. This fraud can go undetected for years as most children do not discover it until years later.

Techniques for obtaining and exploiting personal information for identity theft are numerous and are ever changing, but here are a few:

A. Dumpster Diving—rummaging through rubbish for personal information.

B. Information Technology—retrieving personal data from mobile phones, usb memory sticks, personal computers, and uncleansed hard drives before getting rid of them.
C. Public records—public records about individual citizens published in official registers.
D. Skimming—information from bank or credit card using compromised or hand-held card readers and creating clone cards.
E. Hacking—entering computer networks, systems, and databases to get personal data.
F. Social Media—browsing networks and websites for personal details.
G. Shoulder Surfing—observing users typing log-in or credit card data in public places.
H. Diverting e-mail—to obtain personal information and delay discovery of new accounts opened in the victim's name.
I. Stealing checks—to acquire banking information such as account and routing numbers.
J. Bogus job offers—advertising in order to accumulate resumes for personal data.

Protecting Your Identity

Now that you have gotten a view of what you are up against, let me point out a few things to help protect your individual identity. The first thing you must remember is that guardianship of personal information is vital for intervention strategy, and is recommended by the FTC. Identity related documents such as credit cards, bank statements, utility bills, etc. may be stolen from cars, homes, and offices, or directly from victims by pickpockets and bag snatchers. Secondly, you can really help yourself by not identifying yourself unnecessarily. As a measure of precaution, do not give out your information freely, and always protect yourself against electronic identity theft. Be careful to follow proper protocol to computer and cyber security regulations when purchasing merchandise on-line.

The same is true when it comes to protecting yourself from your spiritual enemy. God's word reminds us to be serious minded and watch for the enemy because Satan is always looking for a way to attempt to steal your identity. Just as the identity thief wants your personal information, so does Satan. If either one gets the information they are after, rough times are ahead. Neither intend to leave you unharmed and will for sure use it against you.

Satan always uses the "bait and switch" tactic where he shows you what seems to look good for you, but you will always come out on the short end of things no matter how good they may appear. Things can turn bad very quickly and then you will start the downward spiral process. Satan not only wants your identity, he wants to clone it so he can assume your daily life, consume your spiritual life, and eventually destroy your eternal life.

Doing business with Satan is always bad business.

Satan will show you riches untold and say you can have it all. The gold he promises you is real, yet it is really fool's gold. In the Bible it teaches us to seek God and His way of doing things first, and then all the other things we need will fall into place (Matthew 6:3).

> *Doing business with Satan is always bad business.*

Satan knows no amount of money is equivalent to the price of your soul. What price would you give in exchange for your soul? Would $40 billion, $60 billion, or $1 trillion be enough? Do you know that Jesus gave His life for it (Mark 8:36-37)?

☙ Key Points to Remember

- ☙ The primary objective of the identity thief is to personally profit at your expense without a hint of remorse or regret for your loss.
- ☙ Satan always uses the "bait and switch" tactic.
- ☙ Doing business with Satan is always bad business.
- ☙ Satan knows no amount of money is equivalent to the price of your soul, but do **you** know it to be true?

Chapter 2
Sexual Mine Field

Satan has been using sex for centuries to cause mankind to fall and steal their identities.

Satan has devised sexual schemes or plans to entice you to participate. However, once you have indulged you will find yourself in a sexual mine field, unable to navigate your way to safety because of all the hidden traps designed to take you out and utterly destroy you (1 Peter 5:8). "How did I get here?" is the question that repeatedly runs across your mind as you search for a way out of danger. Who knew that one moment of unbridled passionate sex would cause all this trouble?

> *Satan has been using sex for centuries to cause mankind to fall and steal their identities.*

Sex is not ugly or nasty nor did God create sex only for procreation. It is to be enjoyed between a husband and wife. It is to be celebrated among married couples, not the unmarried.

When I say married couples, I mean every husband enjoying his own wife, and every wife enjoying her own husband. No spouse swapping or orgies allowed, this is not how God intended it to be.

Just as you would not share your personal data with others for them to use at your expense, do not share your spouse. Marriage is not just a legal document so you can say "I got papers on you." It is a covenant agreement which goes further than the ink on the document; it is to the heart. That is why the word of God tells us to let every man have his own wife, and every wife her own husband (1 Corinthians 7:2). It is a heart-felt agreement between a man and woman which supersedes any other family ties.

You cannot be a momma's boy when you get married. The word of God tells us when we enter a covenant of marriage, the man shall leave his mother and father and cleave (cling) to his own wife (Genesis 2:24). At this point, the wife becomes the number one woman in your life, not mom. The other amazing aspect of the marriage covenant is the godly mathematical equation where $1+1=1$. The two souls and two hearts are joined to create one union called one flesh.

This "one flesh" constitutes more than just the physical union therefore when sex is practiced outside the guidelines in which God intended, it is wrong and it is sin. Sin is missing the mark or guidelines God has prescribed for us to live by, and it hinders our relationship with God, our Heavenly Father. Satan tries to utilize every sinful act to steal our godly identity, kill our witness to the world, and destroy our lives (John 10:10). You have to remember, Satan has lots of experience at doing what he does, and has been doing it longer than you or I have been living. The word of God instructs us to flee fornication because God knows the consequences of it will not end well (1 Corinthians 6:18).

Fornication simply stated is sexual acts among unmarried people, and adultery is sexual acts of married people with someone other than their spouse. Sin alters our identity, and we cannot remain godly if we actively stay in sin, sexual or otherwise. There is a price to pay for getting caught in the sexual mine field. That cost can involve emotional trauma where you cannot seem to get him/her out of my system, and physical trauma which we seem to overlook until it jumps up and bites us in the form of sexually transmitted diseases (STDs).

The Truth about STDs

STDs are sexually transmitted diseases generally acquired by sexual contact. The organisms that cause STDs may pass from person to person in blood, semen, or vaginal and other bodily fluids. Some known STD infections can also be transmitted non-sexually, such as from mother to infant during pregnancy or childbirth, blood transfusions or shared needles. It is possible to contract STDs from people who seem perfectly healthy and who are unaware of being infected. Many STDs cause no symptoms in some people, and some experts prefer the term "sexually transmitted infections." If you are going to be traveling through a sexual mine field, you will need to recognize signs and symptoms.

Sexually Transmitted Infections (STIs) have a range of signs and symptoms. That is why they may go undetected until complications occur or a partner is diagnosed. These are a few of the signs and symptoms that might suggest a STI is present:

- A. Sores or bumps on the genitals or in the oral or rectal area
- B. Painful or burning urination
- C. Discharge from penis or vagina
- D. Unusual vaginal bleeding
- E. Sore, swollen lymph nodes, particularly in the groin area but more widespread
- F. Lower abdominal pain

While this is not the entire list, you certainly should get the idea. I admonish you not to take this lightly, this is serious business! The sooner you know and get treated, the better! Anyone who is sexually active is at risk of exposure to a STI. That is why it is so important for husband and wife to remain faithful within the marriage. Infidelity brings too many extra problems into the relationship. We are already dealing with the daily challenges without adding additional weight to the load of a wedding bliss.

Signs and symptoms of STIs may appear a few days to years after exposure depending on the organism that infected the individual's system. Some symptoms may resolve in a few weeks even without treatment, or progress with later complications or recurrence. In other words, they are unpredictable and require immediate medical attention.

STIs can be caused by bacteria, parasites, and viruses. Know the rules and risks before entering the sexual mine field.

Chlamydia (kluh-mid-ee-uh) is a bacterial STI and affects both men and women. It occurs in all age groups though it is prevalent among young women. You may not know you have it because many people never develop the signs or symptoms. These symptoms may include genital pain and a discharge from the vagina or penis. It is most commonly spread through vaginal, oral, and anal sex. It is possible for a mother to spread Chlamydia to her child during delivery causing pneumonia or a serious eye infection in her newborn. It is not difficult to treat once you know you have been infected. If left untreated, Chlamydia can lead to more serious health problems. Multiple sex partners and infrequent use of condoms are some of the factors that put you at risk to be infected by Chlamydia.

Syphilis is also a bacterial infection and is usually spread by sexual contact. It starts as a painless sore typically on your genitals, rectum, or mouth. It spreads from person to person via skin or mucous membrane contact with the sores. After the initial infection, the syphilis bacteria can lie dormant in your body for decades before becoming active again. So even if you do not detect any trouble, you are not out of danger because it hides deep within the body and you do not know when the attack on your body is going to take place. Early syphilis can be cured sometimes with a single injection of penicillin. Without treatment, it can severely damage your heart, brain or other organs, and can be life-threatening. Although we have advanced in modern medicine, syphilis rates in the United States have been rising since the year 2000, particularly among men who have sex with men.

The genital sores associated with syphilis can make it easier to become infected with the Human Immunodeficiency Virus (HIV) that causes Acquired Immunodeficiency Syndrome (AIDS). Syphilis develops in stages, and symptoms vary with each stage. Primary Syphilis is the first stage, and usually the first sign is a small sore called a chancre (shang-kur). The sore appears at the spot where the bacteria entered the body. While most people only develop one chancre, it is possible for some to develop several.

Primary infection usually occurs about three weeks after exposure. Many who have syphilis do not notice the chancre because it is usually painless and may be hidden within the vagina or rectum. It will usually heal on its own within six weeks; however, with each stage the infection gets progressively worse. Secondary Syphilis may cause you to experience a rash over the entire body, including hands and soles of your feet, and wart-like sores may appear in the mouth or genital area.

Latent Syphilis is referred to as the hidden stage because you have no symptoms. It moves to this stage from secondary due to the neglect of treatment. This stage can last for years with signs and symptoms never returning, or the disease may progress to the tertiary (third) stage. About 15 to 30 percent of people infected with syphilis who do not get treatment will develop complications known as tertiary or late syphilis. At this stage, the disease may damage your brain, nerves, eyes, heart, blood vessels, liver, bones, and joints. These problems may occur many years after the original untreated infection.

Babies born to women with syphilis can be infected with congenital syphilis through the placenta or during birth. This type of infection could cause deafness, teeth deformities and saddle nose (where bridge of nose collapses).

Gonorrhea is a STI caused by bacteria that can infect both males and females. It often affects the urethra, rectum or throat, and in females, it can also infect the cervix. It is passed from one person onto another during sexual contact, including oral, anal or vaginal intercourse. Babies can be infected through childbirth if their mothers are infected. In babies, gonorrhea most commonly affects the eyes, but the symptoms associated with men and women include painful urination, pus-like discharge from the penis or vagina, pain or swelling in one testicle, and pelvic pain. If left untreated, it can cause infertility in men and women, increase risks of HIV/AIDS, and spread through the bloodstream to other parts of your body (eyes, throat, and joints).

Trichomoniasis is a STI caused by a one-celled protozoan, a tiny parasite that travels between people during sexual intercourse. The incubation period between exposure and infection can range from five to twenty-eight days. Men who have it usually have no symptoms. On the other hand, women who have it experience a foul-smelling vaginal discharge, genital itching, and painful urination. To prevent reinfection, both partners should be treated thoroughly with the most common treatment, a mega dose of metronidazole (Flagyl), and avoid unprotected sex until the infection is cured, which takes about a week. Consumption of alcohol within twenty-four hours after taking metronidazole should be forbidden because it can cause severe nausea and vomiting.

Genital Herpes is a common sexually transmitted infection that affects both men and women. It is caused by a virus and usually includes the following symptoms, pain, itching, and sores in your genital area. Many infected people have no signs or symptoms of genital herpes, but can be contagious even if he or she has no visible sores. It is caused by the herpes simplex virus (HSV), with sexual contact as the primary way the virus spreads.

After the initial infection, the virus lies dormant in your body and can reactivate several times a year. There is no cure for genital herpes, but medications can ease symptoms and reduce the risk of infecting others. Condoms can help prevent the transmission of the virus. Recurrences are common, and since genital herpes is different for each person, signs and symptoms may recur off and on for years. Some experience numerous episodes each year while others may experience less frequent outbreaks as time passes. Things such as stress, fatigue, illness, surgery, and menstruation may trigger outbreaks.

Having genital sores increases your risk of transmitting or contracting other STIs, including the AIDS virus. Genital herpes can cause other complications such as meningitis, bladder infections, and rectal inflammation (proctitis), particularly in men who have sex with men. Newborn babies born to infected mothers can be exposed to the virus during the birthing process, which can result in brain damage, blindness, or death.

When HIV/AIDS first surfaced in the United States, it predominantly affected homosexual men. However, we now know that it can be spread through heterosexual sex. Anyone of any age, race, or sexual orientation can be infected. You are at your greatest risk if you have unprotected sex, use intravenous drugs, or are an uncircumcised man. Primary infection phase is where the majority of people infected by HIV develop a flu-like illness within a month or two after the virus enters the body. It may last for a few weeks, and include symptoms of fever, muscle soreness, rash, headache, sore throat, mouth or genital ulcers, swollen lymph glands, night sweats, and diarrhea. Although these symptoms may be mild enough to go unnoticed, the amount of virus in the bloodstream called viral load, is particularly high at this time, and as a result, HIV infection spreads more efficiently than in the clinical latent phase.

During the clinical latent infection, some people have persistent swelling of the lymph nodes; otherwise, there are no specific signs or symptoms. HIV remains in the body as a free virus and in infected white blood cells. It typically lasts eight to ten years, some stay in this stage even longer, but others progress to more severe diseases much sooner. Early symptomatic HIV is when the virus continues to multiply and destroy immune cells. You may develop mild infections or chronic symptoms such as fever, fatigue, swollen lymph nodes, diarrhea, weight loss, cough, and shortness of breath.

If you receive no treatment for your HIV infection, the disease typically progresses to AIDS in about ten years. By the time AIDS develops, your immune system has been severely damaged. HIV destroys CD4 cells, a specific type of white blood cell that plays a large role in helping your body fight disease. Your immune system weakens as more CD4 cells are killed. People infected with HIV progress to AIDS when their CD4 count falls below 200, or experience an AIDS complication such as pneumocystis pneumonia, or tuberculosis. Acquired Immunodeficiency Syndrome (AIDS) is a chronic, potentially life-threatening condition caused by the Human Immunodeficiency Virus (HIV).

HIV interferes with your body's ability to fight organisms that cause diseases by damaging your immune system. It is a sexually transmitted infection, but can also be spread by contact with infected blood, or from mother to child during pregnancy, childbirth or breastfeeding. It can take years before HIV weakens your immune system to the point that you have AIDS. Some other symptoms of AIDS are persistent white spots or unusual lesions on your tongue, blurred and distorted vision, skin rashes or bumps, and shaking chills or fever higher than 100 for several weeks.

There is no cure for HIV/AIDS, but there are medications that can dramatically slow the progression of the disease. These drugs have reduced AIDS deaths in many developed nations, but HIV continues to decimate populations in Africa, Haiti, and parts of Asia.

There are a few steps of prevention to help you avoid or reduce your risk of STIs:

A. Abstain—the most effective way to avoid STIs is to abstain from sex
B. Vaccinations—getting vaccinated early before sexual exposure for some STIs
C. Wait and verify—avoid vaginal and anal intercourse with new partners until you both have been tested for STIs
D. Stay with one—a long term mutually monogamous relationship with a partner who is not infected
E. No A&D—do not drink alcohol excessively or use drugs, you take more risk
F. Circumcision—consider male circumcision to decrease risk of infections
G. Wham/Bam—avoid anonymous casual sex, no online partners or from bars
H. Birds/Bees— becoming sexually active at a young age increases the number of partners and the risk of STIs
I. Wrap Up—use condoms and dental dams consistently and correctly before each sex act

This sexual mine field can steal your health identity and also destroy your life, which is what Satan wants to do all along.

We must remember that his motives are to kill, steal, and destroy. Satan is never our friend. No matter how friendly or peaceful he presents himself, the end is tragedy.

> *This sexual mine field can steal your health identity and also destroy your life, which is what Satan wants to do all along.*

Key Points to Remember

- Satan has been using sex for centuries to cause mankind to fall and steal their identities.
- This sexual mine field can steal your health identity and also destroy your life, which is what Satan wants to do all along.

Chapter 3
Drinking Your Identity Away

Alcoholism is a chronic and often progressive disease that includes problems controlling drinking, being preoccupied with alcohol, and continuing to use alcohol even when it causes problems. Drinking more to get the same effect (physical dependence), or having withdrawal symptoms when you rapidly decrease or stop drinking, are common traits. If you suffer from alcoholism you cannot consistently predict how much you will drink, how long you will drink, or what consequences will occur from your drinking.

It is possible to have a problem with alcohol even when it has not progressed to the point of alcoholism. Problem drinking means you drink too much at times, causing repeated problems in your life, although you are not completely dependent on alcohol. Binge drinking is a pattern of drinking where a male consumes five or more drinks in a row, or a female downs at least four drinks in a row. This can lead to the same health risks and social problems associated with alcoholism. The more you drink, the greater the risks.

The process of becoming addicted to alcohol occurs gradually, although some people have an abnormal response to alcohol from the time they start drinking. Over time, drinking too much may change the normal balance of chemicals and nerve tracts in your brain associated with the experience of pleasure, judgment, and the ability to exercise control over your behavior. This may result in your craving alcohol to restore good feelings or remove negative ones.

There are numerous signs and symptoms of alcoholism, but we will only list a few to show how Satan tries to steal our identity and destroy us in the end:

A. You become unable to limit the amount of alcohol you drink
B. You feel a strong need or compulsion to drink
C. Develop a tolerance to alcohol so that you need more to feel its effects
D. You drink alone or hide your drinking
E. Experience physical withdrawal symptoms like nausea, vomiting, and sweating
F. Have blackouts and cannot remember conversations or comments

G. Have a ritual of having drinks at a certain time and become annoyed if you cannot
H. Keep alcohol in unlikely places at home, at work or in your car
I. Have legal problems or problems with relationships, finance or employment
J. Lose interest in activities and hobbies that used to bring your pleasure
K. There are lots of complications when it comes to dealing with alcoholism.

Alcohol depresses your central nervous system (CNS). However, in some people the initial reaction may be stimulation, but as you continue to drink you become sedated. Alcohol lowers your inhibitions, and affects your thoughts, emotions, and judgment. It affects your speech, muscle coordination, and vital centers of your brain. Heavy drinking could cause a life-threatening coma or death.

Since it can reduce your judgment skills, you are more likely to make poor choices and end up in dangerous situations, or behaviors such as the following:

A. Motor vehicle accidents and other types of accidents
B. Domestic problems
C. Poor performance at work or school

D. Increased likelihood of committing violent crimes
E. Contributes to other deaths like drowning, suicides, and other homicides
F. Teens likely to become sexually active and take more risk in unprotected sex.

The other thing involved in complications with alcoholism is the issue of health. Health problems caused by excessive drinking can include liver disease, digestive problems, diabetes complications, heart problems, birth defects, neurological complications, and a weaken immune system just to mention a few.

Early intervention is the tool of prevention for the fight against alcoholism. The sooner you recognize all the hazards of drinking alcohol before taking that first drink, the better chance you have of not becoming a victim of many not so happy hours in your life. For teens and young people, the likelihood of addiction depends on the influence of parents, peers, and other role models.

It also depends on how much they are influenced by the advertising of alcohol, and how early in life they begin to use alcohol. All the commercials for alcohol lure you into thinking a good time cannot be enjoyed unless you are consuming their product. The truth is, the cameras are not around to show the person's head stuck over the toilet vomiting, or the bodies crushed and mangled inside a vehicle because they were just having a good time having a few drinks. They say "drink responsibly," but when you start drinking sound judgment goes out the window.

Alcohol alters your behavior and ultimately steals your identity.

Alcohol alters your behavior and ultimately steals your identity.

⮞ Key Points to Remember

- Drinking too much may change the normal balance of chemicals and nerve tracts in your brain associated with the experience of pleasure, judgment, and the ability to exercise control over your behavior.
- Alcohol depresses your central nervous system (CNS).
- Alcohol lowers your inhibitions, and affects your thoughts, emotions, and judgment.
- Alcohol affects your speech, muscle coordination, and vital centers of your brain.
- Since alcohol can reduce your judgment skills, you are more likely to make poor choices and end up in dangerous situations or behaviors.
- Alcohol alters your behavior and ultimately steals your identity.

Chapter 4
Suicide

Suicide is the voluntary and intentional act of killing one's self. It robs us of life and causes great pain and emotional trauma to love ones left behind to deal with the tragedy. It is a selfish reaction to a problem or problems we have let Satan deceive us into thinking are so overwhelming that the only way out of the situation is death.

Suicide is another weapon Satan uses to completely take away our godly identity.

When we utilize suicide as a method of escaping life's pressures, we are telling our Heavenly Father that He cannot solve our problems, and that we really do not totally trust Him. What a slap in the face for our Creator when His word plainly says there is nothing too hard for God. Yet we let Satan sucker us into believing our situation is far beyond the reaches of the Creator of the universe.

> *Suicide is another weapon Satan uses to completely take away our godly identity.*

Once we proceed with this method of coping, we never reach our full potential in God. We shorten the life God gave us to accomplish marvelous and wonderful things. We do not just cheat ourselves, we cheat God because we rob Him of the glory that He gets from the things we were meant to accomplish with His help (1 Chronicles 29:11-13).

The Battlefield of the Mind

Satan is always seeking to bombard our minds with all the cares of this life. He wants us to succumb to the pressures of this world and start thinking that there is no hope and no way out of the situations we face every day. After attacking our mental fortress called the mind, he starts tearing away at our faith, trying to get us to doubt our ability to succeed through God's word. If he is able to get us to doubt God's word, then he succeeds in getting us to doubt God.

Our Heavenly Father has said in His word He will never leave us or forsake us, and that the Lord is our helper and we do not need to fear what man tries to do to us (Hebrews 13:5-6). Every temptation has an escape route already built in by God so we are able to deal with the situation and come out victorious (1 Corinthians 10:13). We must continue to operate through our daily activities with the mind of Christ. Jesus never spoke with defeat, not even when facing death on the cross. He spoke triumphantly, and confidently about dying to save mankind and rising from the dead to live again without one shred of doubt.

The choice of life is always better. God did not say that every day would be easy, but He did say He would be with us always, even unto the end of the world (Matthew 28:20). Knowing that our Heavenly Father is with us always and that He will never forsake us gives us the strength to conquer any enemy that tries to steal our identity and to destroy our lives.

Suicide is not an option for our God is greater, and He is the God of life and not death.

Cyber Bullying

Since there has been a great increase in the usage of social media, Satan uses it as another tool help him with suicide attempts. Although there are great things to use social media for, the evil things still lurk about seeking a victim. Cyber bullying is adding another dimension to peer pressure that our youth have to contend with every day. More and more young people are falling under enormous peer pressure from these cyber-attacks and attempting suicide because they feel they have no way out. Being accepted among their peers is very important to them, and not being accepted

Suicide is not an option for our God is greater, and He is the God of life and not death.

is a worse fate than living. They decide to check out of life, not realizing that they have a lot of living left to do.

Thankfully, more young people survive suicide attempts than actually die. Each year approximately 157,000 youth between the ages of ten and twenty-four receive medical care for self-inflicted injuries at emergency departments across the United States. Suicide affects all youth, but some groups are at higher risk than others. For instance, boys are more likely than girls to die from suicide. Of the reported suicides in the ten to twenty-four age group, 81 percent of the deaths were males, and 19 percent were females. However, girls are more likely to report attempting suicide than boys.

Cultural variations in suicide rates also exist with Native American and Alaskan Native youth having the highest rates of suicide-related fatalities. A nationwide survey of youth in grades nine through twelve in public and private schools in the United States found Hispanic youth were more likely to report attempting suicide than their black, white, and non-Hispanic peers.

It is so important to have open communication with our children. They need to feel they can freely come to us without any hesitation with what seem to be overwhelming problems. We need to listen with open ears and hearts before we start spouting off at the mouth without all the facts.

Suicide Hotlines are tools available for our youth and adults. If you start thinking about suicide as a way of escape, you need to get help immediately. Call the hotline numbers, 800-784-2433 or 800-273-8255. There is someone on the line willing to listen to you. There is always a way out without ending your life.

Several factors can put a young person at risk for suicide. However, having these risk factors does not always mean suicide will occur, and some are the same for adults as well:

A. History of previous suicide attempts
B. Family history of suicide
C. History of depression or other mental illness
D. Alcohol or drug abuse
E. Stressful life event or loss
F. Easy access to lethal methods
G. Incarceration
H. Exposure to suicidal behavior of others

Conquering the Overwhelming Pressures of Life

A Christ-like mind is the key to conquering the overwhelming pressures of life.

The mind of Christ does not come by us just saying we have the mind of Christ. We must study God's word to transform our minds into Christ-like minds (Romans 12:2, Philippians 2:5). If Satan can cloud our minds and can cause confusion, we can

> *A Christ-like mind is the key to conquering the overwhelming pressures of life.*

make wrong decisions and start thinking that maybe death is a better option than life. Satan will consistently try to knock us down and keep his foot on our necks, but Almighty God, our Heavenly Father, is there to lift up of our heads if we will allow Him to (Psalms 3:3). We cannot be held down with God on our side.

God is for us and He is more powerful than the whole world that may be coming against us. Our Heavenly Father is the strength of our lives so who or what shall we fear?

Key Points to Remember

- Suicide is a weapon Satan uses to completely take away our godly identity.
- Satan wants us to succumb to the pressures of this world and start thinking that there is no hope and no way out of the situations we face every day.
- Every temptation has an escape route already built in by God so we are able to deal with the situation and come out victorious (1 Corinthians 10:13).
- Suicide is not an option for our God is greater, and He is the God of life and not death.
- A Christ-like mind is the key to conquering the overwhelming pressures of life.
- God is for us and He is more powerful than the whole world that may be coming against us.

Chapter 5
Pride and Arrogance

Pride has good and bad elements. Pride is the good feeling you get from a job well done. Pride is the feeling of great respect for the place where you live as in "Pride in America." Pride can also refer to when you think you are more important or better than everyone else. Pride is that feeling "I am number one" and that is the only number that counts. There is nothing wrong with being confident in whom God created you to be. God put great care into creating the human race (Genesis 1:26-28). We are to think highly of ourselves because we are fearfully and wonderfully made, but not more highly than we ought to think (Romans 12:3). That is where pride becomes a negative instead of a positive.

This is where Satan launches another attack to alter or steal our identity. If Satan can lure us into becoming prideful (getting big-headed), we begin believing and trusting in our own abilities and powers and not God. We become blind-sided by this very pride and our communication with God becomes unclear, although He sends us warnings before destruction comes upon us (Proverbs 16:18, 29:23). This kind of pride is never a good thing. It is self-serving (a legend in your own mind), and destructive.

Satan likes to use the spirit of pride because pride is "Satan's momma," according to Bishop James E. Bolden III of Jacksonville, Arkansas. Before he was Satan, his name was Lucifer, and he was an Arch Angel in heaven. Lucifer's position caused him to allow pride to enter in, and he began to think he was greater than his Creator, God. Lucifer wanted control of heaven and convinced one-third of the angels to follow him. He started an unsuccessful coup in heaven, was defeated, and kicked out (Isaiah 14:12-17). After being booted out of heaven, his appearance and name changed, thus pride birthed forth Satan. Satan realizes that pride can alter or steal your identity from a firsthand perspective and now tries to use it on God's own people.

Pride works the opposite of humility and teamwork. In God's plan of salvation, if you sin or error (2 Corinthians 7:10), you can repent and ask for forgiveness through God's only begotten Son, Jesus Christ, and be restored (2 Peter 3:9). However, pride will not let you humble yourself to ask for forgiveness or acknowledge your fault.

Pride attracts an additional ingredient called stubbornness. Stubbornness is just along for the ride, but often instigates a lot of pride's actions. Because of stubbornness, pride will never back down or humble itself, even when wrong. Neither pride nor arrogance acknowledges weaknesses, and together they gloat in victory. If you do not put pride in check, it can destroy you and everything around you because pride comes before your fall.

Pride and arrogance left unchecked play right into Satan's trap to alter or steal your identity, to kill, or destroy you.

Arrogance goes with pride and are the Siamese twins of bad. Both cause you to think you are better than everyone else. However, arrogance adds insulting behavior or actions that come from thinking you are better, smarter, or more important than others (Proverbs 8:13).

It is better to humble yourself instead of being humbled. That slice of humble pie goes down easier with submission instead of resistance, and the taste is sweeter. Avoiding pride and arrogance is a must to negate the plans of Satan to alter or steal our identity. We must remain humble and totally submit ourselves to God and resist the temptation to become prideful or arrogant. Doing so will frustrate Satan, and he will have to leave and rethink his strategy (James 4:6-7).

> *Pride and arrogance left unchecked play right into Satan's trap to alter or steal your identity, to kill, or destroy you.*

Key Points to Remember

- If Satan can lure us into becoming prideful, we begin believing and trusting in our own abilities and powers and not God.
- Pride will not let you humble yourself to ask for forgiveness or acknowledge your fault.
- Pride attracts an additional ingredient called stubbornness.
- Arrogance adds insulting behavior or actions that come from thinking you are better, smarter, or more important than others.
- Pride and arrogance left unchecked play right into Satan's trap to alter or steal your identity, to kill, or destroy you.
- We must remain humble and totally submit ourselves to God.

Chapter 6
Hypocrisy (Two Faces)

It is important to be who God created you to be. God did not make a mistake in creating you. It does not matter if you are tall, short, thin, medium or large, you are unique and there is no one like you.

Once you realize that you are a designer's original and cannot be duplicated, you begin to love yourself and appreciate your God given gifts and abilities.

Your Word Is Your Bond

> *Once you realize that you are a designer's original and cannot be duplicated, you begin to love yourself and appreciate your God given gifts and abilities.*

There is one thing in life that you will forever be judged, scrutinized, or remembered for and that is your word. Do your actions line up with what you say, or are you a "do as I say, not as I do," type of person? Is your word your bond? If you say it do you do it? Business transactions used to be conducted with a verbal agreement and a handshake. There were no written contracts because your word was the glue that held everything together. Agreements were based on your track record for having integrity in keeping your word. It did not matter if people did not know you personally, the integrity of your word went before you and was known. Does this remind you of anyone in particular?

> *Jesus was known for doing what He said He would do. He is our great example of living without hypocrisy.*

Jesus was known for doing what He said He would do. He is our great example of living without hypocrisy.

Hypocrisy is the behavior of a person who does not do the things that they tell others to do or they do things they tell others not to do. Their actions do not agree with what they claim to believe or feel. This type of behavior makes that person a hypocrite. *A hypocrite is someone who acts in contradiction to his or her stated beliefs or feelings.*

> *A hypocrite is someone who acts in contradiction to his or her stated beliefs or feelings.*

Hypocrisy is another device of Satan in his grand scheme of deception to steal your identity and to annihilate you. He wants you to be double-tongued and profess one thing, but live or do the opposite of what was professed. An example would be a pastor preaching against fornication and adultery, but participating in extra marital affairs outside of the marriage covenant.

We all understand that anyone can falter and error in their decision and make a wrong choice, but it is still sin. The problem is continuing in that sin and not repenting and seeking God's forgiveness. This type of behavior falls into the category of hypocrisy because it does not agree with what one claims to believe or feel.

Satan wants more Christians to become hypocrites because it brings confusion to the body of Christ and the world. If there is no difference in the way Christians live or treat our fellowman then why would others want to make the effort to change? How can we as Christians expect the world to receive Christ when we participate in the same ungodly acts they do?

If the church, the body of believers, does not stand for godly living and show the world a godly example as the right way to salvation, we are all doomed.

> *If the church, the body of believers, does not stand for godly living and show the world a godly example as the right way to salvation, we are all doomed.*

The word of God tells us to come out from among the worldly system and be separated and committed unto God. **Come out from among** them means to stop the ungodly acts. However, **we are to live among** them showing them the right way to live a godly life by being a light to the world. Once we accept Jesus

Christ as our personal Savior and Lord, our lives should reflect that change. We do need to understand that change is progressive and does not necessarily change overnight. There are things in our lives that we need to continue to improve upon.

This is why the Pharisees and Sadducees were upset with Jesus. They were called out by Him for trying to hold the people accountable to the law they did not keep themselves (Luke 12:1). Christians must realize our lives are under scrutiny every day, and someone is always checking to see if you have dotted every "i" and crossed every "t." That is why we must live what we confess.

If we confess to be striving to be Christ-like, then we cannot be abusing our spouses verbally, mentally or physically. Christians cannot agree with the world's view on same sex marriage no matter how politically correct it becomes. In God's plan, a woman was created for a man (Genesis 2:18-25) and marriage is between man and woman; not man and man, nor woman and woman.

As a result, we who profess Christ have done our job if God is glorified, Satan is demoralized, and we will avoid another identity theft.

We must continue to display godly character no matter where we are so that the world will notice. The only Jesus your neighbors, co-workers, family, and friends will see is the Jesus in you (2 Corinthians 3:2-3). As Christians, we must continue to be progressive in our faith walk to let the light of Jesus shine through us providing light to a dark world (Matthew 5:16). When we say what we mean and live what we say, then the world sees a clear picture of Christ that is not distorted or confused.

As a result, we who profess Christ have done our job if God is glorified, Satan is demoralized, and we will avoid another identity theft.

Key Points to Remember

- God did not make a mistake in creating you. Once you realize that you are a designer's original and cannot be duplicated, you begin to love yourself and appreciate your God given gifts and abilities.
- Jesus was known for doing what He said He would do. He is our great example of living without hypocrisy.
- A hypocrite is someone who acts in contradiction to his or her stated beliefs or feelings.
- If the church, the body of believers, does not stand for godly living and show the world by godly example the right way to salvation, we are all doomed.
- When we say what we mean and live what we say, then the world sees a clear picture of Christ that is not distorted or confused.

Chapter 7
Domestic Violence (Love That Hurts)

Love should be shared cherished and enjoyed; it should never and I repeat, never hurt! Domestic violence is a serious threat for both men and women. Physical, verbal, and mental abuse should never be associated with a loving relationship. However, it happens all too often. Although it happens to men as well as women and children, the primary focus today is on the women. Many women today are constant victims of domestic violence or abuse. Battering or intimate partner violence should not occur between people involved in an intimate relationship.

It can take many forms including emotional, sexual, physical abuse, and threats of abuse. Your partner apologizes and says the hurtful behavior will not happen again, but you fear it will. At times you wonder whether you are imagining the abuse, yet the emotional and physical pain you are experiencing is real. If this sounds familiar, you might be experiencing domestic violence.

It might not be easy to identify domestic violence at first. While some relationships are clearly abusive from the outset, abuse often starts subtly and gets worse over time. You might be experiencing domestic violence if you are in a relationship with someone who shows the following signs:

A. *Calls you names, insults you or puts you down*
B. *Prevents you from going to work or school*
C. *Stops you from seeing family members or friends*
D. *Tries to control how you spend money, where you go, what you wear*
E. *Acts jealous, possessive, or constantly accuses you of being unfaithful*
F. *Threatens you with violence or a weapon*
G. *Forces you to have sex or engage in sexual acts against your will*
H. *Hits, kicks, shoves, slaps, chokes or otherwise hurts you, your children or pets*
I. *Blames you for his or her violent behavior or tells you that you deserve it*

If you are lesbian, bisexual or transgender, you might also be experiencing domestic violence. If you are in a relationship with someone who threatens to tell friends, family, colleagues or community members your sexual orientation or gender identity, that is abuse. Although these sexual lifestyles are contrary to God's word, no one deserves this type of abuse. God does not hate the person. God dislikes the sin committed by the person.

Domestic violence has no regards of race or sexual preference, we all bleed red.

Domestic violence steals your identity because you cannot be yourself when involved with an abusive spouse or partner. They will not let you because they want to dominate every aspect of your life.

Husbands are to love their wives as Christ loved the church, and gave Himself for it (Ephesians 5:25). That is a tall order, but one worth trying to fulfill. If husbands love their wives like Jesus loved the church, they would love, provide, cherish, protect, communicate, and be willing to give their lives for their wives. Fulfilling that directive from the word of God would eliminate violence among the married sector. It would also serve as a marriage role model to the single sector on how to be treated in a marriage relationship.

Domestic violence has no regards of race or sexual preference, we all bleed red.

If he does not open doors for you nor bring flowers for no special reason during the courtship, he is probably not going to during the marriage. One of the mistakes many women make is that they think they can change the behavior of their partner once they are married. This is not a reasonable expectation. In fact, more often than not the negative behavior escalates once a couple is married.

You do not have to stay in an abusive relationship. You should leave as soon as possible and get to a safe place first, and then get help for you and your partner. There are domestic violence hot lines to call. They will give guidance on how to proceed. Staying in an abusive relationship only robs you of your identity, and that is not what God wants for you.

Key Points to Remember

- Domestic violence has no regards of race or sexual preference, we all bleed red.
- Domestic violence steals your identity because you cannot be yourself when involved with an abusive spouse or partner.
- Negative behavior during courtship often escalates after marriage.
- Leave abusive relationships, seek safety, and then get help for you and your partner.

Chapter 8
Hamartiology

Hamartiology is the study of sin. It derives from the Greek word *hamartia*. Sin means missing the mark or established guideline. It is considered a deliberate violation of God's will according to Judaism and Christianity. It is looked upon as moral evilness from a religious viewpoint. Sin disconnects or interrupts the covenant relationship with Almighty God. True repentance of sin is an admission of wrong doing with regret and godly sorrow. It is a change in one's heart, mind, and behavior. Unless true repentance takes place the relationship cannot be mended or continued. If you are truly sorry, you will make a 180 degree turn from that sin with a noticeable change in behavior. When the people of God repented, God restored the relationship and forgave their sins (violations of His law).

What does this have to do with identity theft? In order to understand Satan's tactics, you have to know about his history or his mode of operation. As part of his plan to steal Adam and

Eve's identity and authority, he needed a diabolical scheme. He could not just show up saying give me your authority on earth, and the lease that goes with it.

How many of us would give the keys and deed to our property if a perfect stranger showed up at our home and asked for them? I dare say none of us would do such a thing. Satan had to trick and deceive Adam and Eve into forfeiting their authority by disobedience to God (Genesis 3:1-24). Satan did not make them do it, he only presented an opportunity.

Remember, the fish only gets caught if it takes the bait. So resist the bait (temptation) Satan has adorned his trap with and you will avoid the heartaches and pain of succumbing to sin. Doing this will allow you to experience and enjoy victory over Satan's plan of identity theft. It is a feeling of euphoria for a Christian to stand strong in the power of God's might and daily defeat Satan's snares through obedience to God.

Obedience to God's word and God's way is an essential key to avoiding satanic identity theft.

Key Points to Remember

- Satan had to trick and deceive Adam and Eve into forfeiting their authority by disobedience to God.

- Resist the bait (temptation) Satan has adorned his trap with and you will avoid the heartaches and pain of succumbing to sin.
- Obedience to God's word and God's way is an essential key to avoiding satanic identity theft.

Chapter 9
Demonology

We talked about sin and the final results of sin, so now let's talk about the satanic agents behind the scene of sin called demons. Demonology is the systematic study of demons or evil spirits, or beliefs about demons. They are agents of evil and their primary objective is to cause harm, distress, or ruin. Demons take orders from their boss, Satan, the kingpin of evil and wickedness. His motto is to "steal, kill, and destroy."

> *It is important to know your enemy, and what his plans are concerning you.*

It is important to know your enemy, and what his plans are concerning you.

God has an enemy. His name is Satan and he hates everything about God. His only problem is that he cannot defeat God, so he goes about with his devious and diabolical plans to try and destroy God's creation, mankind. Satan was not always evil. His name was Lucifer and he was an Arch Angel that resided around the throne of God. His name meant "Morning Star." He got filled with pride and arrogance, and led an unsuccessful revolt against God, the Creator of all. For his actions, God booted Lucifer and the other angels that joined him out of heaven. Therefore they are referred to as fallen angels or demons.

Lucifer is no more, but Satan is and he is very real and very angry for getting booted out of heaven. These fallen angels are no longer agents of good, but of evil. Demons or evil spirits do not have a physical body. Therefore, they require a human being or physical body to operate here on earth.

Satan is trying to steal the identities of Christians and he has enlisted the help of his little side-kicks the demons to accomplish this task. Understand, neither Satan nor his demons are up to any good. As a matter of fact, they despise anything that is good like health, prosperity, love, peace, and all the things that pertain to God. Satan and his crew like to appear as if they are good for you, but in the end when it is too late we find out it was a lie. We are left in situations of sickness, poverty, despair, hatred, and even death just to name a few. The whole plot is a clever illusion by Satan and company to destroy us. However, the truth is he is a liar and the originator of all lies (John 8:44).

Satan does not just want to humiliate us, he wants to rub salt in our wounds, kick us when we are down, put his foot on our necks, twist the knife as he is stabbing us, and finally laugh in our faces as he enjoys watching us take our last breath at the point of death. Make no mistake, Satan wants to destroy everyone and everything associated with God. It does not matter to him who or what he uses as long as it gets the job done.

It would seem that we are up against an undefeatable opponent and the outcome is one of despair. Be encouraged, God has given us the tools to handle this thief and it is called the word of God, the Holy Bible. It is filled with godly wisdom and knowledge pertaining to strategies for dealing with our identity thief and his crew of despicable demons. In the word of God we are told how tenacious and determined Satan is and to be on watch (1 Peter 5:8). God also tells us we will receive some blows (never known a boxer that has not been hit), but to endure or "shake it off" and stay focused. God will strengthen us and give us the victory, but we must remember to give only Him the glory and the credit for doing so (1 Peter 5:9-11).

Deception and Illusions

Deception is the art of making someone believe something that is not true. This person is called a deceiver. Identity thieves must use deceptions and illusions to be successful in obtaining their goals. They are very persistent and do not give up easily. This describes Satan who is often referred to as the deceiver.

The identity thief has to create an illusion to make someone believe something that is not true. It could be obtaining a driver's license or credit card in the victim's name and using it for personal profit. Satan wants to deceive the world into believing he does not exist, and that God is to blame for all the bad things that happen in the world.

To some degree he has done his job. We are quick to ask, "Why did God let this happen to me?" What we need to stop and realize is that Satan and company have been at work 24/7 trying to make our life a living hell (Job 1:6-7). Satan is good at what he does and has over 2,000 years of experience in the deception department.

Illusion is one of his best weapons. They appear to be real, but when examined closely they are all smoke and mirrors. If Satan can convince the world God is to blame for the earthquakes, tsunamis, massive floods, increasing poverty, and seemingly needless death and destruction, then he can cause us to focus on the attacks and not the attacker. This is his way of driving a wedge between man and God.

Satan wants mankind to curse God and die (Job 1:8-12). He wants us to turn our backs on our Creator and forfeit our inheritance, which is eternal life (Romans 6:23). He wants to steal our identity as children of God (John 1:12, 1 John 3:2). This is something Satan will not have again and is forever trying to rob us of ours.

The words *jealous*, *envious*, and *hatred* all describe Satan's attitude toward the children of God. He wants our identity. Do not be deceived, study God's word, and become equip to battle that old identity thief called Satan (2 Timothy 2:15).

Key Points to Remember

- It is important to know your enemy, and what his plans are concerning you.
- Make no mistake, Satan wants to destroy everyone and everything associated with God. It does not matter to him who or what he uses as long as it gets the job done.
- The Bible is filled with godly wisdom and knowledge pertaining to strategies for dealing with our identity thief and his crew of despicable demons.
- Satan wants mankind to curse God and die (Job 1:8-12).
- Satan wants us to turn our backs on our Creator and forfeit our inheritance, which is eternal life (Romans 6:23).
- Satan wants to steal our identity as children of God (John 1:12, 1 John 3:2).

Chapter 10
Christology

Christology is the study within Christian theology which is concerned with the nature and person of Jesus Christ as recorded in the Holy Scriptures. It is also concerned with the relationship of Jesus and God the Father. In Christology we try to understand the ministry of Jesus to observe His acts and teachings to get a clearer picture of His role in salvation.

Better understanding of Jesus Christ and His ministry is a vital key to understanding His work against Satan, the identity thief.

Satan came to steal, kill, and to destroy, but Jesus came to undo the works of Satan (1 John 3:8). In other words Jesus came to give life, health and abundance, not death, sickness and poverty (John 10:10). Jesus and Satan have been rivals for a long time. Jesus saw Lucifer get kicked

> *Better understanding of Jesus Christ and His ministry is a vital key to understanding His work against Satan, the identity thief.*

out of heaven by His Heavenly Father (Isaiah 14:12) and is well acquainted with the tricks of Satan, the identity thief.

Looking at the life of Jesus through the Holy Scriptures, we will ask three questions and attempt to provide information that shows Jesus is more than capable of stopping that identity thief called Satan.

Why was Jesus born?
Why did Jesus have to die?
Why did God resurrect or raise Jesus from the dead?

As Christians we do not have to take being bullied and abused by Satan. It is our choice to let Satan run over us and take what he wants, when he wants, how he wants, and then laugh in our faces as we cry about it.

When we play the role of the victim, we are walking right into the trap of losing our identity of who we are—the victors, not the victims. We are more than able to defeat Satan at his game through Jesus Christ (Romans 8:37-39). Christ means "the anointed one," it was not Jesus' last name. It is a personification of who He is.

Why was Jesus born?

Jesus was born to undo the works of Satan. Satan, by deception, tricked Eve and Adam into disobedience, and caused them to sin by eating fruit from the tree of knowledge of good and evil. God had already instructed them not to eat from that particular tree. When they disobeyed and ate the fruit which God told them not to, it caused them to sin, and allowed sin to rule over man.

By disobeying God, Adam let Satan steal his identity or position with God.

Beforehand, Adam walked and talked with God, and there was a close relationship between them. Adam and Eve were created in God's image, not the physical body, but the spiritual being dwelling inside (Genesis 1:26-27). When sin entered the relationship it caused a gap between humanity (mankind) and God.

> *By disobeying God, Adam let Satan steal his identity or position with God.*

Sin is a stench unto His nostrils. Adam and Eve had dominion over all the earth until sin entered the equation and Satan stole the keys. Jesus was born to right everything that went wrong because of the decisions of our earthly parents, Adam and Eve.

Why did Jesus have to die?

Due to sin, mankind would have been lost and eternally separated from God had Jesus not volunteered to sacrifice Himself for humanity past, present, and future. Jesus had to die to redeem mankind from the clutches of sin. He is still undoing the shady works of that thief Satan. Adam and Eve were the original creation of God and they knew no sin. They were the spiritual image of God. They were holy and undefiled. However, once sin entered through them the original became flawed.

God told them to be fruitful and replenish the earth, meaning have children. In reproduction, if your original has a flaw then every copy will have the same flaw, no matter how many times you reproduce it. In essence, every child born unto Adam and Eve and their descendants would be born into sin because the original seed was tainted. We were doomed if it had not been for God's plan of redemption.

Jesus left His heavenly home to enter this world through a virgin birth. He became like us, putting on an earth suit, and living a sinless life for thirty-three years. Then He went to the cross to die for the sins of the world. Jesus did all of this because He shared the same love for mankind that His Heavenly Father had (John 3:16). God's plan for redeeming man is so advanced and so awesome, you cannot really fathom it all.

God takes a virgin named Mary and has the Holy Spirit overshadow her, and impregnates her with a holy unblemished seed. See where this is going? The first Adam's seed was tainted due to sin. Now Jesus, who is referred to as the second Adam, is holy and undefiled. All who come after Him are godly seeds or children of God thereby restoring the relationship (Romans 8:14, 17).

Jesus is the last Adam because there will never be another like Jesus; therefore He is Alpha and Omega, the beginning and the end. He was there in the beginning, He will be there in the end when it is all over, and He is also here now in the present providing victories over that thief Satan. By one man, Adam, sin entered into the world (Romans 5:12). By the sacrifice of one man, Jesus, sin is forever defeated (Romans 5:19).

When sin entered this world through the disobedience of Adam and Eve, it required blood to cover or atone for that sin (Genesis 3:21).

From that moment, designated animal sacrifices were required for the temporary atonement (payment of damages) of our sins. Mankind caused a rip or tear in our relationship with God our Creator. There had to be bloodshed for the remission and forgiveness of sin (Hebrews 9:22) as ordained by God. The animal sacrifice had to be healthy without spot or blemish to even be considered worthy of being sacrificed. This was symbolic of a temporary cleansing which had to be done continuously. God, our Heavenly Father knew that the blood from bulls, goats, sheep, and turtle doves was not final.

When sin entered this world through the disobedience of Adam and Eve, it required blood to cover or atone for that sin (Genesis 3:21).

No sacrifice was truly unblemished and sin free until Jesus arrived. He offered His life in exchange for the penalty of our sins. We now know that the penalty for our sins is death (Romans 6:23), but we gain the gift of eternal life through Jesus Christ.

Why did God resurrect or raise Jesus from the dead?

While the death of Jesus and the shedding of His blood paid the penalty for our sins, His resurrection—being raised from the dead, is the proverbial cherry on top of the sundae. It was a crowning moment that would forever (eternally) change the destiny of all mankind (1 Peter 1:3). No longer would we have to continue with animal sacrifices for the temporal cleansing of sin (Hebrews 9:12-14). Jesus, the sinless Lamb of God, was sacrificed once and covered sins past, present, and future. God the Father had to raise His only begotten Son from the dead to complete the salvation plan, and to keep His promise of a redeemer for fallen man.

We had to continuously sacrifice for the payment of sin because the ultimate sacrifice, Jesus, God's only Son, had not yet arrived on the scene to give His life for the remission (cancelling) of sin. The resurrection of Jesus accomplished what animal sacrifices could not. He paid the final debt for sin once and for all (for eternity). Animal sacrifices are no longer required because none could compare to the sinless Lamb of God, who gave His life and defeated sin in the flesh.

How could one sacrifice make amends when thousands were not enough? First, Jesus shed His blood and gave His life for our sins (Leviticus 17:11). Secondly, Jesus died in our place. He knew no sin but became sin for us. Jesus took our punishment for us so we would not have to. Since there was no sin in Him, the blood was, and still is pure, spotless, and without blemish unlike that of animal sacrifices. Next, when the penalty was paid and the sacrifice was dead, Jesus was raised, is alive, and lives forever more.

Blood was shed, the penalty for sin paid, and the Lamb of God was resurrected with all power. Since Jesus is alive and empowered, so is the blood He shed on the cross. The blood is alive and still has power to cleanse and save today. The blood of Jesus will never lose its power. It has been over 2,000 years, and the blood of Christ still works.

There is no more need for animal sacrifices. However, there is a need for human sacrifices. Not the taking of human life, but the dedication of human life for receiving redemption from sin. Since we owe a debt we cannot pay, and Jesus paid a debt He did not owe, we are indebted to Him for restoring life to us. A life for a life is the only right thing to do, but God will not force us to submit our lives to Him. We must of our own free will choose to do so. By surrendering our lives unto God for His service, we become holy instruments (witnesses) of the Most High God through His Son, Jesus.

Jesus suffered and died a cruel humiliating death by crucifixion for our sins. All He is asking us to do is to believe in Him, live our lives according to the word of God, the Holy Bible, and share this wonderful experience with others. That is not too difficult of a request when compared to our other option—death. I am not a betting man, but I like my odds with Jesus. No matter what the situation or circumstance, my rate of success is 100 percent with Jesus in my corner. The harder the problem is the more God shows Himself strong. There really is nothing too hard for God!

You can read all the terms and definitions about Jesus that you want, but it is not until you get to know Him personally that you begin to understand the love He has for you. You will begin to experience a relationship that is second to none. It is first class all the way, God does not do or make anything second class. His way is beyond superb.

On the other hand, Satan is always trying to duplicate or out do what God has done. If Satan cannot outperform what God has established, he tries to steal it or alter its original godly function, aka identity theft. He can only do it if we let him gain entry into our lives by doing the opposite of God's word.

Jesus defeated Satan and his plan to destroy mankind by dying on the cross and paying sin's ransom for restoration for mankind with His blood. Jesus justified us with His resurrection from the dead and is alive forevermore. We are victorious over the identity thief and his bag of tricks when Jesus is Lord over our lives. He never slumbers nor sleeps, but is always watching on our behalf, and giving us warning after warning when the thief is in our neighborhood. We are to be alert and vigilant.

⚷ Key Points to Remember

- ⚷ Better understanding of Jesus Christ and His ministry is a vital key to understanding His work against Satan, the identity thief.
- ⚷ When we play the role of the victim, we are walking right into the trap of losing our identity of who we are—the victors, not the victims.
- ⚷ By disobeying God, Adam let Satan steal his identity or position with God.
- ⚷ When sin entered this world through the disobedience of Adam and Eve, it required blood to cover or atone for that sin (Genesis 3:21).
- ⚷ God will not force us to submit our lives to Him. We must of our own free will choose to do so.
- ⚷ We are victorious over the identity thief and his bag of tricks when Jesus is Lord over our lives.

Chapter 11
Soteriology

Soteriology is the study of the biblical doctrine of salvation. It comes from two Greek terms, *soter* meaning "savior" or "deliverer," and *logos* meaning "word." Salvation, as we know in the biblical sense, deals with deliverance from the stronghold of sin or redemption. It also refers to deliverance from danger, an oppressor, or foe, thus being saved or rescued (Psalms 27:1-6, 61:1-4). It is the latter explanation that connects with identity theft.

If you have ever been given assistance during an automobile mishap such as a flat tire, or dropped money without knowing it and someone returned it to you, then you have a general idea about salvation. Identity theft violates that safe haven. It is a horrible crime that leaves a wide path of destruction for the victims. It can become quite an overwhelming task to put your life back together after experiencing such an ordeal.

My first reaction was one of total surprise when my financial institution call center inquired about a credit card transaction that happened internationally while I was still in the United States. After a thorough investigation I was able to avoid that charge, but they struck again for $250.00 later the same day. After speaking with the call center, they immediately inactivated that card and placed my account on fraud alert.

Secondly, I was emotionally angered, mad as heaven, and I wanted to repeatedly lay hands on every thief involved, and not in the name of Jesus. The next thing was a feeling of helplessness, followed by frustration. I strongly desired to catch the culprit, but did not know how. Where does he or she live? Who do I contact? There were so many questions and so few answers on the horizon.

My financial institution was aware of the situation, the immediate inactivation of the card, and an issue of an emergency card for my account allowed me to try and get back to normal daily living. I was informed that I needed to file a theft report with the local police department, and bring a copy of the report back to my financial institution as proof so I could begin the process of recovering my stolen funds.

It takes everyone working together to bring justice to your situation. No doubt about it, you need to be saved from the identity thief. Remember, the thief comes to steal, kill, and to destroy. He steals your personal data, kills your checking and savings accounts, and destroys your credit and your good name.

Salvation, in its own way, is the equalizer to identity theft. Satan comes to steal our true identity, and cause a separation in the relationship between us and God by enticing us to sin. Once Satan gets us entangled in the bondage of sin we feel guilty, and overwhelmed by the situations or events in which we are involved. Sometimes it seems as if there is no way out, and that all hope is lost. It is the kind of hopeless feeling you get when you realize your identity has been compromised. Please realize there is still hope, and you can overcome. The answer is by salvation through Jesus Christ.

Jesus did this through His death, burial, and resurrection. With His death Jesus paid the penalty for our sins (2 Corinthians 5:21). His burial sealed that sin in a closed file never to be opened. Satan tries to get into the file and remind us of our past and attempts to use the past as a weapon to steal our godly identity of who we are now. Jesus' resurrection erased the whole file and gave us a new start in life (2 Corinthians 5:17).

The sin which separated us from our Heavenly Father has been washed away by the blood of Jesus, and we have now been restored to our original identity as living images of the only true and living God (Genesis 1:26-28). This gift called salvation is for all according to John 3:16-17. Since it is a gift, God will not force us to accept it, we must of our own free will accept the gift of salvation.

Faith ignites this reunion with our Heavenly Father for it is simply strong belief. Strong belief that God sent His only Son Jesus to die for our sins, and that Jesus was resurrected by His Heavenly Father after three days with all power to conquer sin, death, hell, and the grave. As we strongly believe this, an internal process is taking place, and the identity thief, Satan, is evicted from taking illegal refuge within us. Our true godly identity is restored. When we strongly believe, and repent or turn away from ungodly behavior, and go in the opposite direction which is toward God, our Heavenly Father welcomes us back into the family.

Excited as I was when my financial institution restored the funds I had lost through identity theft, I was and still have an exuberance of joy from receiving salvation through Jesus Christ. Now that I know my true identity, Satan can no longer trick me about sins in my past. Old things are no more because God has thrown them in the sea of forgetfulness.

Our past is not who we are because our lives are forever changed through Jesus. Our future looks good.

⚭ Key Points to Remember

- ⚭ Satan always tries to get into the file and remind us of our past and attempts to use the past as a weapon to steal our godly identity of who we are now.

- Jesus' resurrection erased the whole file and gave us a new start in life (2 Corinthians 5:17).
- Our past is not who we are because our lives are forever changed through Jesus. Our future looks good.

Chapter 12
Eschatology

Eschatology is the study of what will happen when all things are consummated at the end of history, especially focusing on the Second Coming of Christ. The word eschatology comes from two Greek words, *eschatos* which means last and *logos* which in this case means study. It is then referred to as "the study of last things." I like to say, God will have the last word. It is important to know our Christian history so we will not repeat the mistakes of our Christian forefathers. The knowledge of sins past and present should allow us to gain a better relationship with our Heavenly Father through His Son, Jesus Christ.

Since this is the study of last things, God allows us to get a glimpse of the future when evil and all of God's enemies are put down once and for all. It lets us know that with Christ we are more powerful than the world against us, and that no weapon formed or orchestrated by Satan against us shall prosper. There will be peace and no more sin. It means that sin's by-products, sickness, disease, and poverty will also be destroyed. We will have an unobstructed true holy relationship with our Heavenly Father, the way God planned it from the beginning.

This brings us back to Satan being a great identity thief. He used his wiles in the Garden of Eden to deceive Eve and caused Adam to disobey God's instructions thereby illegally gaining Adam's authority or dominion over this earth. Although Satan tricked Adam and Eve in the Garden to steal their identity and authority, he still does not have legal rights to operate here on earth.

Adam and Eve had physical bodies or earth suits to live on earth, Satan did not because he is a spirit. That is why he must utilize other human beings and animals to do his dirty work. We are in a continuous battle with Satan, but the word of God tells us that the weapons of our warfare are not carnal. We cannot fight spirit with flesh. So our weapons are mighty through God to the pulling down of strongholds (2 Corinthians 10:3-4).

Satan hates God, and he will use anyone and anything to try to get revenge on God. He knows he cannot defeat God because he already tried and was kicked out of heaven. Satan knows he is on borrowed time, and he tries to enact his revenge on God by trying to destroy mankind, especially those of us that call ourselves Christians (Christ-like).

This battle between good and evil has been an ongoing saga throughout centuries. God's plan has been progressively traveling through time until God says "time is up." God's plan for redemption and restoring His relationship with mankind was created, and completed before the foundations of the world (Ephesians 1:4) were laid.

Eschatology tells us the conclusion of the whole matter when God has the last word. Satan has deceived and inflicted his terror on this world long enough, and God will put this identity thief in his proper place. He is going down! It is only befitting that our Creator, our Heavenly Father, has the last word because in the beginning was the Word, and the Word was with God. All things were created by Him that was created (John 1:1).

God spoke which means words came forth and the universe was created. We know that the Word was and is Jesus, His Son. God had the first word, and He is going to have the last word, the final say so. All of the identity thief's lies, tricks, and destruction are going to put to an end in the final judgment. Satan is going to pay for all the things he has done to God's people throughout the ages. If this was a chess match, it would be check mate and time to pay the piper.

Since Jesus is the author (John 1:1) and finisher (John 19:30) of our faith, He has given us insight through His word what Satan's end will be according to Revelation 20:10. No longer will he be allowed to torment, oppress, and possess people. All the things he used to keep this world in turmoil like racism, hatred, sexual sins, greed, pride, poverty, sickness, and disease will stop. God the Alpha (beginning) and God the Omega (end) has already penned the outcome of what is to come, His will, His way, the last say.

Key Points to Remember

- It is important to know our Christian history so we will not repeat the mistakes of our Christian forefathers.
- With Christ, we are more powerful than the world against us, and no weapon formed or orchestrated by Satan against us shall prosper.
- We cannot fight spirit with flesh so our weapons are mighty through God to the pulling down of strongholds (2 Corinthians 10:3-4).
- Since Jesus is the author (John 1:1) and finisher (John 19:30) of our faith, He has given us insight through His word what Satan's end will be according to Revelation 20:10.

Chapter 13
Think—A Brain Snack

"Time waits for no one," I once heard so we must make the most of the precious time given to us during our lifetime. We cannot afford to squander it, thinking by some chance that we can make it up or redeem it. God is the only one who can transcend time, and make something better than it was originally because He is the Ancient of Days. God is here now, has been, and always will be here because He created everything including time, the segments of life we travel through daily.

God has a plan for us, and we do not have time to waste. That plan is sharing the good news called the gospel to the world that they might come to know our Heavenly Father through His Son Jesus. He wants all to become children of God through His holy adoption, and enjoy a wonderful relationship with the Creator of the universe, our Father.

Time is of the essence because Satan knows that his time is running out, and that his judgment is coming soon. He is going to be cast into a lake of fire with intense heat and pain unimaginable. Satan wants people to accompany him on his way to the lake of fire. He does not want to be alone on this trip because unlike a normal day with twenty-four hours, time will have no end. It is called eternity. Eternity means forever and ever, there is no end. God created time for our benefit that we might have a reference point to the segments of our daily lives. We are to use this time to glorify Him while we remain on this earth. When time ends as we know it that is when eternity begins.

Everyone will have an eternity, but where will you spend it? The word of God tells us that after death comes the judgment or giving accountability for your actions with the time given you while on earth. You do not just die and that is it. God has so much more in store for His children. There is an inheritance for those who lived accordingly to God's word, and who used time wisely to glorify and give Him a return on His investment in us called life. We cannot allow Satan to steal our identity because our inheritance called eternal life is at stake. He does not want us to realize it until it is too late.

Once we enter into eternity there is no redeeming of time, so we must prepare before that time comes. Jesus told us that we would not know the day nor hour when He would return to gather the children of God together and take us home to be with our Heavenly Father, but we are to be ready. Satan wants to knock us off course and cause us to detour and miss our glorious trip to heaven.

Satan has a variety of tools or tricks he likes to use. These are Satan's weapons for mass destruction, but I call them brain snacks or food for thought. We must study the word of God to store it in our memory to be able to conquer the weapons of Satan. In our thought process we must stay focused on the word of God, and not the weapon Satan is trying to use on us.

Think about being victorious over these weapons:

- *Racism*
- *Hatred*
- *Segregation*
- *Murder*
- *Suicide*
- *Genocide*
- *Homosexuality*
- *Lesbianism*
- *Greed*
- *Pride*
- *Reprobate Mind*
- *Mental Disorders*
- *Domestic Violence*
- *Adultery*

- *Fornication*
- *Alcoholism*
- *Drugs*
- *Sex Trafficking*
- *Political Corruption*

We are more than capable of defeating Satan when he comes against us. Jesus left us the blue print of success to defeat him. Have you read it lately? It is the word of God.

Bibliography of References

www.merriam-webster.com/dictionary

www.wikipedia.org

www.justice.gov

www.cdc.gov

www.mayoclinic.com

www.thefreedictionary.com

www.britannica.com

Chafer Theological Seminary www.chafer.edu

www.hebrews4christians.com

www.consumer.ftc.gov/identitytheft

United Churches of God www.ucg.org

Nelson's New Illustrated Bible Dictionary, 1995 edition, editor: Ronald F. Youngblood

www.wikipedia.org/wiki/identity_theft

The Holy Bible, King James Version/ Amplified Bible Parallel Edition, 1995, Zondervan

Bolden, James E., Bishop, January 1, 2013

www.suicide.org

About the Author

Gene A. Rhodes is a native son of Arkansas. He is a twenty-one-year military veteran who now resides in Jacksonville, Arkansas, and is an Assistant Pastor in a local community church. He is also a loving husband and father, and along with his wife Elnora, they have six children and eleven grandchildren. Gene believes that Christians of today have to make a more concerted effort to maintain godly standards that reflect our identity with Christ and not that of the world, and continue to be a beacon of light to a dark world. We must continue to show Christ-like behavior so that others may recognize their loss and reclaim their true identity from Satan through Jesus Christ. Amid all the changes in the world today, there remains one constant element, His name is Jesus.